DyslexiaGames.com

Creative Copywork

Learn to Write Well by Copying Familiar Rhymes.

45 Fun Lessons

The Most Natural Way for Children to Learn is by Copying Others.

These familiar childhood rhymes will condition your child's mind to writing well.

The Thinking Tree

The Thinking TREE

www.DyslexiaGames.com

Dyslexia Games Series B –Book 8
Friendly Copyright Notice:

The Thinking Tree LLC ● 617 N Swope St. ● Greenfield, IN 46140 ● info@dyslexiagames.com ● +1 317-622-8852

Creative Copywork

Learn to write well by coping poetry and rhymes.

By Sarah J. Brown
& Anna Brown

Parent Teacher Instructions:

**This book provides your child with a transition
from reading games to schoolwork, if your child struggles with this book repeat
Books B-2, B-3 and B-6, and then come back to this one later.**

Provide the student with a pencil, eraser, and a set of sharp colored pencils, if he wants to color in the pictures.

1. Read each poem with your child twice.
2. Study the picture together.
3. On the next page the child will need to fill in the missing words.
4. The last exercise is copying a section of the poem. Make sue the child doesn't misspell or skip any words. Check for periods and capital letters. Their finished work should match the original poem perfectly. If there are any mistakes, show the child what is wrong and require the child to start over. Once the child has to rewrite the lesson a time or two she will be very careful to make it just right next time.

Your child may think that these rhymes are just for little kids. We chose these because we know that many children know these rhymes already. By reading and writing familiar rhymes your child will be able to comprehend the literature more easily, and will need less help from the teacher. If any of the rhymes are new to your child, read them together a few extra times.

Hey Diddle Diddle

Hey <u>diddle</u> diddle,
The cat and the <u>fiddle</u>,
The cow <u>jumped</u> over the moon,
The little dog laughed to <u>see</u> such sport,
And the dish ran <u>away</u> with the Spoon.

Name:_____   **Date:**_____

Hey Diddle Diddle

Hey _____ diddle,
The cat and the _____,
The cow _____ over the moon,
The little dog laughed to _____ such sport,
And the dish ran _____ with the Spoon.

Name:_____ Date:_____

Hey Diddle Diddle

Hey diddle diddle,
The cat and the fiddle,
The cow jumped over the moon,
The little dog laughed to see such sport,
And the dish ran away with the Spoon.

Name:_____ **Date:**_____

Hey diddle diddle,

_____

_____

The cat and the fiddle,

_____

_____

The cow jumped over the moon,

_____

_____

The little dog laughed to see such sport,

_____

_____

And the dish ran away with the Spoon.,

_____

_____

Name:_____ Date:_____

Jack and Jill

Jack <u>and</u> Jill
Went <u>up</u> the hill
To fetch a <u>pail</u> of water,
Jack <u>fell</u> down
And <u>broke</u> his crown
And Jill came <u>tumbling</u> after.
Up <u>Jack</u> got
And home <u>did</u> trot
As <u>fast</u> as he could caper,
Went <u>to</u> bed
To mend his <u>head</u>
With vinegar and <u>brown</u> paper.

Name:_____ **Date:**_____

Jack _____ Jill
Went _____ the hill
To fetch a _____ of water,
Jack _____ down
And _____ his crown
And Jill came _____ after.
Up _____ got
And home _____ trot
As _____ as he could caper,
Went _____ bed
To mend his _____
With vinegar and _____ paper.

Jack and Jill

Jack and Jill
Went up the hill
To fetch a pail of water,
Jack fell down
And broke his crown
And Jill came tumbling after.
Up Jack got
And home did trot
As fast as he could caper,
Went to bed
To mend his head
With vinegar and brown paper.

Name:_____   **Date:**_____

Copywork

Jack and Jill went up the hill

_____

_____

To fetch a pail of water,

_____

_____

Jack fell down and broke his crown

_____

_____

And Jill came tumbling after.

_____

_____

Name:_____ **Date:**_____

Peter Piper

Peter Piper picked a peck of pickled peppers.
A peck of pickled peppers Peter Piper picked.
if Peter Piper picked a peck of pickled peppers,
Where's the peck of pickled peppers Peter Piper picked?

Name:_____ **Date:**_____

Peter Piper

Peter Piper _____ a peck of pickled peppers.
A peck of picked _____ Peter Piper picked.
If Peter Piper picked a peck of _____ peppers,
Where's ____ peck of pickled peppers _____ Piper picked?

Name:_____ **Date:**_____

Peter Piper

Peter Piper picked a peck of pickled peppers.
A peck of pickled peppers Peter Piper picked.
If Peter Piper picked a peck of pickled peppers,
Where's the peck of pickled peppers Peter Piper picked?

Name:_____ Date:_____

Peter Piper picked a peck of pickled peppers

_____

_____

A peck of pickled peppers Peter Piper picked?

_____

_____

If Peter Piper picked a peck of pickled peppers,

_____

_____

Where's the peck of pickled peppers Peter Piper picked?

_____

_____

_____

Name:_____ **Date:**_____

Hushaby

Hush-a-bye, don't you cry,
Go to sleep my little baby.
When you wake you shall have
All the pretty little horses.
Black and bays, dapples and grays,
All the pretty little horses.
Hush-a-bye, don't you cry,
Go to sleep my little baby.

Name:_____ Date:_____

Hushaby

Hush-a-bye, _____ you cry,

Go to _____ my _____ baby.

When you _____ you _____ have

All the _____ little horses.

Black and _____, dapples and_____,

All the _____ little _____.

Hush-a-bye, don't _____ cry,

Go to _____ my little baby.

Name:_____ Date:_____

Hushaby

Hush-a-bye, don't you cry,
Go to sleep my little baby.
When you wake you shall have
All the pretty little horses.
Black and bays, dapples and grays,
All the pretty little horses.
Hush-a-bye, don't you cry,
Go to sleep my little baby.

Name:_____ Date:_____

Name:_____ **Date:**_____

I Had a Little Nut Tree

I had a little nut tree,
Nothing would it bear
But a silver nutmeg,
And a golden pear;
The King of Spain's daughter
Came to visit me,
And all for the sake
Of my little nut tree.

Name:_____ **Date:**_____

17

I Had a Little Nut Tree

I had a little nut tree,

_____ _____ _____ _____

But a silver nutmeg,

_____ __ __ _____ _____ ;

The King of Spain's daughter

_____ _____ _____ _____ ,

And all for the sake

_____ __ _____ _____ _____ .

Name:_____ **Date:**_____

I Had a Little Nut Tree

I had a little nut tree,
Nothing would it bear
But a silver nutmeg,
And a golden pear;
The King of Spain's daughter
Came to visit me,
And all for the sake
Of my little nut tree.

Name:_____   Date:_____

I Had a Little Nut Tree

_____

_____

_____

_____

_____

_____

_____

_____

_____

_____

_____

_____

Name:_____ **Date:**_____

I Saw A Ship

I saw a ship a-sailing,
A-sailing on the sea.
And, oh, but it was laden
With pretty things for thee.

There were comfits in the cabin,
And apples in the hold;
The sails were made of silver
And the masts were made of gold.

Name:_____ **Date:**_____

I Saw A Ship

I saw a _____ a-sailing,
A-sailing _____ the sea.
And, oh, _____ it _____ laden
With pretty _____ for thee.

There _____ comfits _____ the cabin,
And _____ in the hold;
The sails _____ made of silver
And _____ masts _____ made of gold.

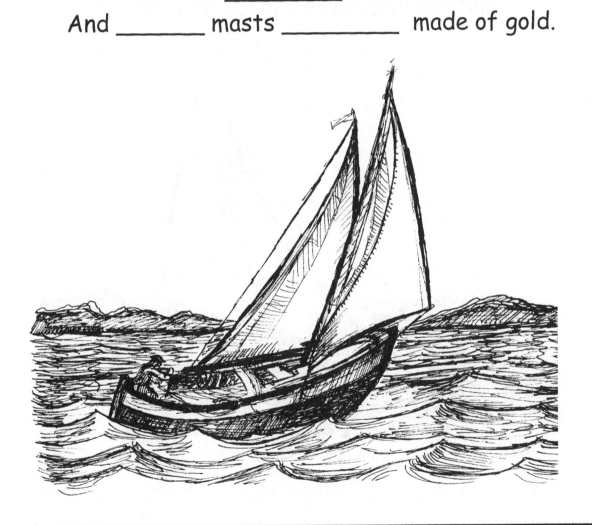

Name:_____ Date:_____

I Saw A Ship

I saw a ship a-sailing,
A-sailing on the sea.
And, oh, but it was laden
With pretty things for thee.

There were comfits in the cabin,
And apples in the hold;
The sails were made of silver
And the masts were made of gold.

Name:_____ **Date:**_____

I Saw A Ship

_____

_____

_____

_____

_____

_____

_____

_____

_____

_____

_____

_____

Name:_____ **Date:**_____

One Two Buckle My Shoe

One, two,
Buckle my shoe;
Three, four,
Knock at the door;
Five, six,
Pick up sticks;
Seven, eight,
Lay them straight:
Nine, ten,
A big fat hen;

Name:_____ Date:_____

One Two Buckle My Shoe

One, _____,
Buckle _____ shoe;
_____, four,
Knock ____the door;
Five, _____,
Pick ____sticks;
Seven, _____,
Lay _____ straight:
Nine, _____,
A big fat _____;

Name:_____ **Date:**_____

One Two Buckle My Shoe

One, two,
Buckle my shoe;
Three, four,
Knock at the door;
Five, six,
Pick up sticks;
Seven, eight,
Lay them straight:
Nine, ten,
A big fat hen;

Name:_____ Date:_____

One Two Buckle My Shoe

_____

_____

_____

_____

_____

_____

_____

_____

_____

_____

_____

_____

Name:_____ **Date:**_____

The Market Square

I had a penny,
A bright new penny,
I took my penny
To the market square.
I wanted a rabbit,
A little brown rabbit,
And I looked for a rabbit
'Most everywhere.

For I went to the stall where they sold sweet lavender
("*Only a penny for a bunch of lavender!*").
"Have you got a rabbit, 'cos I don't want lavender?"
But they hadn't got a rabbit, not anywhere there.

Name:_____   **Date:**_____

I had a penny,
And I had another penny,
I took my pennies
To the market square.
I did want a rabbit,
A little baby rabbit,
And I looked for rabbits
'Most everywhere.

And I went to the stall where they sold fresh mackerel
("*Now then! Tuppence for a fresh-caught mackerel!*").
"Have you got a rabbit, 'cos I don't like mackerel?"
But they hadn't got a rabbit, not anywhere there.

Name:_____ Date:_____

I found a sixpence,
A little white sixpence.
I took it in my hand
To the market square.
I was buying my rabbit
I do like rabbits),
And I looked for my rabbit
'Most everywhere.

So I went to the stall where they sold fine saucepans
(*"Walk up, walk up, sixpence for a saucepan!"*).
"Could I have a rabbit, 'cos we've got two saucepans?"
But they hadn't got a rabbit, not anywhere there.

Name:_____ **Date:**_____

I had nuffin',
No, I hadn't got nuffin',
So I didn't go down
To the market square;
But I walked on the common,
The old-gold common...
And I saw little rabbits
'Most everywhere!

So I'm sorry for the people who sell fine saucepans,
I'm sorry for the people who sell fresh mackerel,
I'm sorry for the people who sell sweet lavender,
'Cos they haven't got a rabbit, not anywhere there!

Name:_____ **Date:**_____

The Market Square

I had a _____,
A bright new penny,
I took my penny
To the _____ square.
I wanted a rabbit,
A little brown _____,
And I _____ for a rabbit
'Most everywhere.

For I went to the stall where they sold sweet lavender
("Only a penny for a bunch of lavender!").
"Have you got a rabbit, 'cos I don't want lavender?"
But they hadn't got a rabbit, not anywhere there.

Name:_____ Date:_____

I _____ a penny,
And I had another penny,
I took _____ pennies
To the market square.
I did _____ a rabbit,
A little _____ rabbit,
And I looked for rabbits
'Most everywhere.

And I went to the stall where they sold fresh mackerel
(*"Now then! Tuppence for a fresh-caught mackerel!"*).
"Have you got a rabbit, 'cos I don't like mackerel?"
But they hadn't got a rabbit, not anywhere there.

Name:_____ Date:_____

I _____ a sixpence,
A little white sixpence.
I took it in my _____
To the market square.
I was _____ my rabbit
I do like rabbits),
And I looked _____ my rabbit
'Most everywhere.

So I went to the stall _____ they sold fine saucepans
("*Walk up, walk up, sixpence for a saucepan!*").
"Could I have a rabbit, 'cos we've got _____ saucepans?"
But they hadn't got a _____, not anywhere there.

Name:_____ **Date:**_____

I _____ nuffin',
No, I hadn't got nuffin',
So I didn't go down
To the _____ square;
But I walked on the common,
The old-gold _____...
And I saw _____rabbits
'Most everywhere!

So I'm _____ for the people who sell fine saucepans,
I'm sorry for the _____ who sell fresh mackerel,
I'm sorry for the people who _____ sweet lavender,
'Cos they haven't _____a rabbit, not _____ there!

Name:_____ Date:_____

The Market Square

I had a penny,
A bright new penny,
I took my penny
To the market square.
I wanted a rabbit,
A little brown rabbit,
And I looked for a rabbit
'Most everywhere.

For I went to the stall where they sold sweet lavender
("Only a penny for a bunch of lavender!").
"Have you got a rabbit, 'cos I don't want lavender?"
But they hadn't got a rabbit, not anywhere there.

Name:_____ Date:_____

_____

_____

_____

_____

_____

_____

_____

_____

_____

_____

_____

_____

_____

Name:_____ **Date:**_____

I had a penny,
And I had another penny,
I took my pennies
To the market square.
I did want a rabbit,
A little baby rabbit,
And I looked for rabbits
'Most everywhere.

And I went to the stall where they sold fresh mackerel
("Now then! Tuppence for a fresh-caught mackerel!").
"Have you got a rabbit, 'cos I don't like mackerel?"
But they hadn't got a rabbit, not anywhere there.

Name:_____ Date:_____

_____

_____

_____

_____

_____

_____

_____

_____

_____

_____

_____

_____

_____

Name:_____ **Date:**_____

I found a sixpence,
A little white sixpence.
I took it in my hand
To the market square.
I was buying my rabbit
I do like rabbits),
And I looked for my rabbit
'Most everywhere.

So I went to the stall where they sold fine saucepans
("*Walk up, walk up, sixpence for a saucepan!*").
"Could I have a rabbit, 'cos we've got two saucepans?"
But they hadn't got a rabbit, not anywhere there.

Name:_____ **Date:**_____

Name:_____ **Date:**_____

I had nuffin',
No, I hadn't got nuffin',
So I didn't go down
To the market square;
But I walked on the common,
The old-gold common...
And I saw little rabbits
'Most everywhere!

So I'm sorry for the people who sell fine saucepans,
I'm sorry for the people who sell fresh mackerel,
I'm sorry for the people who sell sweet lavender,
'Cos they haven't got a rabbit, not anywhere there!

Name:_____ **Date:**_____

Name:_____ **Date:**_____

Name:_____ **Date:**_____

_____

_____

_____

_____

_____

_____

_____

_____

_____

_____

_____

_____

_____

Name:_____ **Date:**_____

_____

_____

_____

_____

_____

_____

_____

_____

_____

_____

_____

_____

_____

_____

_____

Name:_____ **Date:**_____

47

Creative Copywork

Certificate of Completion

_____

Name & Age

_____

Date of Completion

The Thinking
TREE

_____

Dyslexia Games

_____

Teacher

Creative Copywork

Learn to write well
by copying familiar rhymes.

I saw a _____ a-sailing,
A-sailing _____ the sea.
And, oh, _____ it _____ laden
With _____ things for thee.

45 LESSONS
"Finally, a fun solution for reading confusion!"

Made in United States
Orlando, FL
23 February 2024

43659948R10030